Let's Learn About…

ORANGUTANS

By: Breanne Sartori

Introduction

The orang-utan is a very special animal!
They are very big but also very caring.
Unfortunately they are also almost extinct.
These animals are highly intelligent and are
closely related to humans. They are easily
recognised by their long orange hair and
big round faces.

What is an Orang-utan?

Do you know the difference between a monkey and an ape? An ape doesn't have a tail and is a lot bigger. Orang-utans are apes that live in the trees. They are very closely related to humans when you look at their DNA!

What Orang-utans Look Like

Orang-utans have very shaggy and long red hair all over their bodies. Their legs and arms are very long. Their face, hands and feet are covered in thick black skin. Males also develop big cheek pads and a throat pouch.

Size

Orang-utans are huge animals! They are about 5 feet tall when standing fully upright. That's almost as tall as an adult human! They weigh as much as an adult human too – up to 200 pounds!

Arms

Orang-utans have very impressive arms. They are so long that when they stand up, their hands almost drag along the ground! Their arm span is about 7 feet long. Their arms are ridiculously strong too!

Hands and Feet

Our hands and feet are used for different things. Orang-utan hands and feet can do the same things! They are equally dexterous, which is a hard word meaning that they are as useful as each other. Both their hands and feet can be used to hold things or even use tools!

Where Orang-utans Live

Orang-utans are only found on two small islands, Borneo and Sumatra. Both of these islands are in south east Asia where it is very warm. They live high in the trees of jungles and forests in the hills, near swamps and even high in the mountains.

Nests

Orang-utans build themselves nests in the tree tops. They use folded branches and leaves to make padding so that they're comfortable. When it's raining they even use big leaves as umbrellas to stay dry!

Territory

Each orang-utan has their own territory. It is big enough that they can move in different seasons to where they know different types of plants grow. They don't mind too much if other orang-utans are in their territory though. They don't like to fight.

Moving About

Because apes are so heavy they can't move through the trees by jumping like monkeys do. Instead they swing from branch to branch. Their arms are long and powerful enough that they can move between trees without needing to get onto the ground.

Social Life

Orang-utans aren't social animals at all! They love to be by themselves and usually only see each other when mating. Mothers and their babies are different and have a very special bond. They will stay with each other all day until the baby is old enough to be alone.

Communication

In general orang-utans are really quiet. The males make rumbling sounds when moving through the trees to warn others to get out of its way or just to let others know he is there. During mating season the male makes howling noises to attract females.

What Orang-utans Eat

Orang-utans are omnivores, which means that they eat both meat and plants. It is very rare for orang-utans to eat meat though. Sometimes they have insects, but most of the time they eat fruits and plants. They even eat bark!

Getting Water

Orang-utans are geniuses! When it is dry season (which means it doesn't rain much) it can be hard to find water. To fix this, orang-utans make sponges out of chewed-up leaves to soak up water droplets in little cavities in the tree branches!

Baby Orang-utans

Baby orang-utans are very dependent on their mothers. They spend most of their time clinging onto their mothers as they move through the trees and eat. They are even dependent on their mother's milk until they are 3 years old!

Breeding

Female orang-utans only give birth to one live baby at a time. Their babies are born in nests high in the trees. Because females only give birth every 8 years, they will only have about 3 children in their lifetime.

The Life of an Orang-utan

The orang-utan has a pretty quiet and slow life. Baby orang-utans live with their mothers until they are 8 years old. Even then they aren't ready to have their own babies until they are at least 12 years old! It is lucky that they live until they are 30-40 years old.

Predators

Despite their huge size and the fact that they live in trees, orang-utans aren't safe from predators. Tigers, clouded leopards and crocodiles are the main predators of orang-utans. Occasionally an Asian black bear can hunt them too.

Other Dangers

Unfortunately orang-utans are critically endangered. This means that they are very close to being extinct. This is because humans have been clearing the forests they live in so they have no where to live anymore. Sometimes they are killed so that their babies can be stolen and sold illegally as pets.

Bornean Orang-utan

The Bornean Orang-utan is the more common of the two species and even has three sub-species. You can't tell the difference just by looking at them though. Bornean orang-utans are bigger than their Sumatran cousins.

Sumatran Orang-utan

The Sumatran Orang-utan is much hairier than the Bornean orang-utan! Not only is their hair longer, it's much more reddish in colour. The Sumatran orang-utan is much more endangered than the Bornean species – as few as 3,000 are thought to be left in the wild!

Made in the USA
San Bernardino, CA
27 September 2016